A Pocket Guide to Starting a Freelance Business

A Pocket Guide to Starting a Freelance Business

Dakota Frandsen

Bald and Bonkers Network Academy

CONTENTS

CONTENTS

Disclaimer:
This pocket guide has been crafted for informational purposes only. While every effort has been made to ensure the completeness and accuracy of the content, there may be inadvertent errors in typography or content. Additionally, the information presented in this pocket guide is accurate only up to the publishing date. As such, this guide should be viewed as a helpful resource rather than an exhaustive reference.
The primary objective of this pocket guide is to provide educational insights. The author and the publisher do not guarantee that the information contained herein is entirely comprehensive and shall not be held responsible for any errors or omissions. The content is intended to serve as a guide, offering valuable information and perspectives.
It is essential to note that the author and publisher do not assume liability or responsibility for any person or entity concerning any loss or damage, whether direct or indirect, caused or alleged to be caused by the information presented in this pocket guide. Users are encouraged to exercise their judgment and seek additional resources if needed.
In summary, this pocket guide aims to empower and educate, but users should use their discretion and consider seeking professional advice where appropriate. The dynamic nature of the subject matter may render some information subject to change, and users are encouraged to verify details independently.

Welcome

So, you find yourself at the crossroads, contemplating the enticing world of freelancing. Is it the allure of freedom, flexibility, and the ability to chart your own course that beckons you? Starting a freelance business isn't just a career move; it's a life-altering decision that reshapes not only your professional trajectory but also your entire outlook on work.

While freelancing offers unparalleled liberation, it's not for the faint of heart. Contrary to the misconception that it's as straightforward as rolling out of bed and firing up your laptop, freelancing demands dedication and effort. It's not a mere shortcut to monetize your hobbies; it's a legitimate career path that requires genuine commitment.

Yet, the rewards of freelance work are nothing short of extraordinary. It's about stepping out of your comfort zone, embracing rejection as a natural part of the journey, and actively seeking opportunities. Remember, the worst anyone can say is "no," and the real shame lies in not trying at all.

Freelancing can be pursued in various forms – part-time, as a side hustle, or evolving into a full-time profession over time. This comprehensive eBook is your indispensable resource, equipping you with the tools you need for a successful freelancing venture. It doesn't just scratch the surface; it delves into the common challenges, answers the burning questions new freelancers often have, and unveils the unique perks that come with the freelance lifestyle.

The first section serves as the cornerstone of your freelance career. It encourages you to visualize your dream life, aiding in determining if free-lancing aligns with your aspirations. Stressing the importance of meticulous planning, it emphasizes that freelancing isn't a realm where you can im-provise as you go along. Thorough research and planning are the keys to success – understand your service, industry, and audience before taking the plunge.

Beyond planning, goal setting, and legal consid-erations, the eBook explores the paramount role of a compelling portfolio. It provides actionable tips on effectively populating your portfolio to attract your target audience. Additionally, it delves into the challenge of starting in the field without an extensive track record, weighing the pros and cons of various platforms for finding freelance work.

Time management and recognizing the value of your work are pivotal aspects of freelancing. This pocketguide underscores the importance of understanding that your time is a valuable asset, influencing your overall work-life balance.

Finally, the guide concludes by shedding light on potential avenues for business expansion once you've achieved a certain level of success. As a future freelancer, this ultimate guide isn't just a roadmap; it's your passport to navigating the intricate landscape of starting a freelance business and embarking on a transformative journey. Dive in, absorb the insights, and let the exhilarating adventure of freelancing unfold before you!

What are the Basics?

Is freelancing the right path for you? The answer likely echoes through the pages of this pocket guide, and if you're here, you're already leaning towards a resounding "yes"! Starting a freelance business demands a blend of courage and investment, two qualities you're showcasing by immersing yourself in this content.

Discover Your Unique Skill Set:

Now, let's navigate the landscape of your skills. Consider the diverse talents you've accumulated over the years—from your formal education to hands-on experiences. Your freelance journey is poised for success when you harness these strengths. Think of your skills as the building blocks that will shape the foundation of your business.

Passion Matters:

Beyond skills, the heartbeat of your business lies in your interests. What sparks joy in your daily life? Dive into your passions and hobbies. Understanding what truly excites you will guide you towards projects that not only pay the bills but also bring fulfillment. Your business thrives when it aligns with your genuine interests.

Reflect on Your Best Work:

Take a stroll down memory lane and reflect on your past projects. Identify the elements that made certain endeavors enjoyable. Was it the collaborative spirit of a team, the satisfaction of customer service, or perhaps the creative freedom you experienced? Learning from your positive experiences is instrumental in shaping the trajectory of your freelance career.

Define Your Services Clearly:

Moving on, it's time to define your services. What will you offer, and equally important, what won't you offer? Clarity in your service offerings ensures that you channel your energy into tasks that not only showcase your expertise but also resonate with your passion. This clear definition will be the compass guiding your business decisions.

Explore Freelance Business Ideas:

The freelance realm is a vast canvas waiting for your unique brushstrokes. As you consider your venture, here's a curated list of potential niches that align with various skill sets and interests. Remember, these are just starting points; the beauty of freelancing lies in the ability to tailor your services to your strengths and passions.

1. Writing:

- Copywriting
- Editing
- Proofreading
- Blogging
- Journalism
- Ghost-writing
- Content writing

2. Web Development:

- Web design
- Website creation
- Software programming

3. Design and Creativity:

- Graphic design
- Photography

4. Communication Services:

- Transcribing
- Translating

5. Educational Services:

- Teaching

- Online English teaching
- Tutoring

6. Digital Marketing:

- Social media marketing
- Content creation
- Brand management
- Search Engine Optimization (SEO)

7. Administrative and Support Services:

- Data entry
- Admin
- Bookkeeping
- Virtual assistant

8. Marketing and Branding:

- Marketing strategy
- Brand consulting

Once you've explored these broad categories, consider narrowing down to a specific niche that resonates with you. Specialization not only sets you apart but also attracts clients seeking expertise in a particular area. Your chosen niche can evolve as your skills and direction change, offering flexibility in shaping your freelance identity.

Remember, this list is just the tip of the iceberg. Feel free to blend skills from different categories, creating a unique blend that reflects your individuality. The freelance landscape is yours to explore and mold—let your creativity and passion guide you as you embark on this exciting journey!

Understanding Your Clientele:

With your services defined, turn your attention to your potential clients. Who are they? Delve into the details of your target market. Quality triumphs over quantity, so be discerning in your client selection. While it may be tempting to accept every opportunity, remember that you have the power to say no. Cultivate long-term relationships with clients who align with your values and vision.

Unveiling Hidden Costs:

As you set sail on your freelance journey, be

prepared for hidden upfront costs. Assess your industry requirements and evaluate the tools and resources you need. Do you require new software or technology? Will you be working from home or renting a workspace? Even a coffee shop office comes with its costs (think coffees and snacks!). Anticipating these expenses in advance prevents unwelcome financial surprises down the road.

Mastering Self-Motivation:

Freelancing ushers in a new era where you are your own boss. Embracing this autonomy requires self-motivation and discipline. No longer tethered to a manager demanding more, you must set your own pace. Recognize your worth in the freelance landscape; feeling undervalued can quickly lead to a lack of motivation. Discover what motivational strategies work best for you and weave them into your routine to conquer your goals.

In this dynamic landscape of freelancing, each step is a building block towards your success. Now, armed with a deeper understanding, let's forge ahead and uncover more gems on this exciting journey!

| 12 |

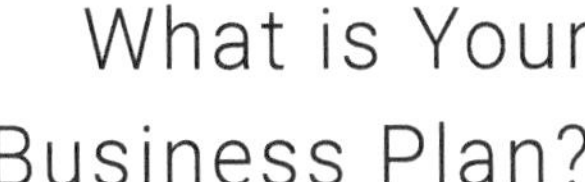

3

What is Your Business Plan?

Creating A Business Plan And Choosing Your Goals:

Embarking on the freelance journey demands more than just talent—it requires a strategic approach. A business plan is your compass, guiding you through the intricate landscape of freelancing. While an exhaustive fifty-page document isn't necessary (unless that suits your style), a concise collection of goals is indispensable.

In the realm of business plans, countless templates might overwhelm you with complicated sections. As a freelancer, focus on distilling your main goals, those that resonate with both your business and personal aspirations. Think of it as a personalized map, a reference point to navigate the unpredictable waters of freelancing.

Moreover, your business plan is not a static artifact. As your business evolves, so should your goals. Regularly set aside time for reflection and updates, ensuring your plan remains relevant and aligned with the trajectory of your freelance career.

Setting Clear Goals:

Before delving into the intricacies of your business plan, take a moment for introspection. Why do you want to embark on this freelance adventure? Understanding the motivation behind your decision will empower you to maximize your potential.

Are you considering freelancing as a side gig or envisioning it as a full-time career? Uncover the essence of your freelance motivation—whether it's to escape the daily commute, embrace entrepreneurial independence, supplement your income, or achieve a harmonious work/life balance.

This exploration lays the foundation for your goals. What do you seek to achieve as a freelancer? Let your thoughts flow freely, writing down everything that comes to mind. This exercise becomes the cornerstone of your business plan, shaping it around your unique aspirations.

Considerations Before Starting:

A critical aspect of crafting your business plan involves a realistic evaluation of your financial landscape. Calculate the cost of living, considering not only your freelance income but also any other revenue streams. Transitioning to freelancing may involve a temporary pay cut, so it's vital to prepare and plan for this adjustment.

Determine your ideal income level, a pivotal factor influencing your pricing strategy, working hours, and project load. Acknowledge the shift from a steady paycheck to intermittent income—a transition that comes with its challenges, such as following up with clients for payments.

Moreover, outline your desired wage in your business plan. This benchmark becomes a reference point, a metric to gauge your progress periodically. If you find yourself falling short, delve into the reasons and realign your goals accordingly.

Research and Understanding:

Knowledge is your greatest ally as a freelancer. Before setting sail, research your industry and understand your competition. Success in the freelance world demands setting yourself apart, and the best way to achieve this is through understanding.

Regularly monitoring your competition is not just a one-time task—it's an ongoing process. Avoid stagnation by periodically checking in on your competitors, understanding their successes, and learning from their mistakes. This continual research ensures your services remain current and in demand.

Creating Your Brand:

In the evolutionary journey of your freelance business, a defining moment arrives when you must carve out your personal brand. Your brand is the lens through which your target clientele views your business—it's a badge of professionalism and authority, a key indicator of business success.

The visual elements of your brand are crucial. This encompasses your business name (which could simply be your own), your logo, aesthetic design elements, and the stylization of your website or portfolio. Beyond the visual, your brand encapsulates the overarching goals and missions of your business.

Crafting a compelling brand is not a one-size-fits-all process. It's a dynamic endeavor, one that may evolve with your business. Integrating your brand into your business plan provides a clear framework for maintaining consistency and relevance.

Where to Find Clients:

Understanding your target market is the bedrock of a successful freelance business. After defining what your business will offer, assess whether there's a sufficient client base to sustain it. While there's usually a market for almost everything, it's wise to ensure there are enough clients genuinely interested in your services.

Demographically defining your target market is essential. Dive deep into understanding their behavior. Where do they look for freelancers? What is their online presence like? This nuanced understanding is pivotal for effective targeting. Without a solid understanding of your audience, your business might struggle to find its footing.

In essence, comprehending your audience enables you to tailor your services to meet their specific needs and preferences. This strategic alignment is a powerful tool for attracting and retaining clients.

Utilizing Your Business Plan:

Your business plan isn't a static document gathering dust on a shelf—it's a dynamic tool to navigate the ebbs and flows of freelancing. Equip your future self with inspiration by incorporating practical elements into your plan.

Include a list of potential client ideas and places to find clients. During dry spells, refer back to these ideas, reaching out to pitch your services and revitalize your workflow. Create a catalog of dream projects; when time allows, work on these projects to reignite your passion and expand your portfolio.

Moreover, compile a list of marketing strategies to implement during slow periods. Discover new avenues to target clients, expanding your business reach and client pool. And when inspiration wanes, having a curated list of "things to do when you do not know what to do" can be a game-changer. It's a roadmap to reignite your spark and propel your freelance business forward.

Defining Your Mission Statements or Goals:

Refining your business plan to encapsulate mission statements or clear goals is a valuable exercise. These statements can be aspirations or guides on how you want to conduct your business. Keep them within easy reach for regular reminders, ensuring your business aligns with your envisioned path.

Remember, your business plan is not set in stone; it's a living document. Regularly update it to reflect the evolution of your business. Stagnation is not a sign of success in freelancing; growth and adaptability are key indicators of a thriving freelance enterprise. Embrace change, update your plan as needed, and let your freelance business flourish in the ever-evolving landscape.

4

Are You Operating Legally?

The Legal Stuff: Taxes, Ethics, And Contracts

Embarking on the legal aspects of freelancing may seem like navigating a labyrinth, but neglecting them can lead to potential pitfalls. While it might not be the most thrilling part of your freelance journey, understanding the legal landscape is crucial for the longevity and success of your business.

Legalities:

Legal requirements for freelance businesses vary from state to state, making thorough research imperative. Broadly, you'll need to consider aspects such as tax registration, business registration, company structure, and ownership. Additional insurance might be necessary, especially if you plan to work from home—some home insurance policies might not cover business activities.

Delve into intellectual property laws, exclusivity clauses, credit policies, data protection concepts, and conflict of interest resolutions. Being proactive about legal considerations will save you from potential legal troubles down the road. Remember, when it comes to the law, being proactive is more advantageous than being reactive.

Business Ethics:

Beyond legality, there's a realm of ethics that freelancers must navigate. What is legal might not always align with what is ethical. As a business owner, your behavior and reputation are paramount. Upholding ethical standards is not just a choice; it's a safeguard for your business.

Demonstrate dependability, productivity, open-mindedness, and compliance. Maintain integrity and loyalty in your interactions. Communication is key; keep clients informed of your progress and involve them in the process. Adhering to realistic project deadlines and transparent communication builds trust.

Avoid shortcuts and unethical practices. Remember, your behavior reflects on your business, and maintaining a professional image is crucial, even if you're working in your pajamas.

Contracts:

Contracts are your shield in the freelance world, defining expectations and protecting both parties involved. Clearly outline terms, such as the number of revisions, payment expectations, project details, and deadlines. Payment terms, whether hourly or lump sum, should be explicitly stated.

Creating a template for your terms and conditions streamlines the process, but tailor it as needed. Contracts serve as a defense against clients seeking additional work without additional payment. Trust your instincts but ensure legal protection. Contracts, when used correctly, can save you from legal complexities by clearly outlining your terms, requirements, and expectations.

In essence, the legal and ethical dimensions of freelancing are not mere formalities; they are the foundation of a sustainable and reputable business. Approach them with diligence, seeking professional advice when needed, and pave the way for a thriving freelance venture.

5

Working with Little Experience?

How To Start Working With Little Experience: Overcoming Challenges

Embarking on a freelancing journey with limited experience can be both exciting and challenging. The transition to a form of work that is often inconsistent and uneven may seem daunting, but with the right strategies, you can build a successful freelance career. This chapter explores effective methods for starting freelance work when you are just getting started.

Gaining Experience First: A Gradual Approach

Many seasoned freelancers recommend against an immediate shift from full-time regular work to becoming a full-time freelancer. Instead, consider gaining experience gradually. Starting part-time allows you to build experience alongside other work commitments. This approach provides a safety net, allowing you to secure your footing in the freelance world before making it your sole source of income.

Working on building your experience in your spare time sets the stage for a more secure transition into full-time freelancing. There's no shame in starting part-time; for some, it offers valuable insights into the lifestyle and responsibilities of freelancing while maintaining the security of additional income.

Working for Free: Balancing Act

Working for free can be a tempting way to gain experience and populate your portfolio, but it's

crucial to strike a balance. While it can be a beneficial strategy for some, it might not work for everyone. It's important to be cautious about working
for free, as it can sometimes lead to a devaluation
of your skills.

Exposure, while valuable, doesn't pay the bills.
If working for free aligns with your financial situation and contributes to building your portfolio, it
might be a viable option. However, it's essential to
be mindful of potential pitfalls and ensure that the
benefits outweigh the drawbacks.

Work for Less: Understanding Value

Starting with lower rates is a practical approach
for freelancers with little experience. This strategy
helps you gain initial reviews, attract clients, and
add projects to your portfolio. By working for a
lower wage initially, you gain a better understanding of the true value of your work.

Moreover, working for less can serve as a valuable introduction to the freelance lifestyle. It allows

you to adjust to the demands of freelancing, determine the time required for project completion, and refine your pricing strategy based on your newfound insights.

Gaining Clients: Building Long-Term Relationships

Client retention should be a primary focus when starting your freelancing business. Initially, you may not have a roster of existing clients, but that can change. Every interaction or project should aim to build a lasting client relationship. Encourage satisfied clients to recommend your services to others, expanding your network organically.

By understanding your target audience, you can proactively seek and retain clients. Building a database of clients over time allows you to tailor your services to their needs and preferences. Client relationships are a cornerstone of a successful freelance business.

Cold Contacting and Pitching: Proactive Outreach

While cold contacting is typically discouraged in sales, for freelancers, it can be a proactive strategy. Initiating contact with potential clients demonstrates initiative and can positively position your brand. Learning how to pitch your services effectively is crucial in making a lasting impression.

Research potential clients, tailor your pitch to their specific needs, and present an irresistible offer. Putting yourself out there, especially if you offer competitive pricing, is an effective way to gain experience and build long-lasting client relationships.

Be Confident: Key to Success

Confidence plays a pivotal role in freelancing success. If you project uncertainty or lack conviction in your services, potential clients are likely to mirror that sentiment. Boosting your confidence can be achieved through skill-enhancing courses relevant to your field.

Consider taking courses to bolster your professionalism, making you appear more skilled and qualified. If uncertainty lies in the business side of freelancing, finding a mentor or building a network of freelancers can offer valuable guidance. Networking with those in similar industries or locations can help navigate the legal aspects of your business and provide specific advice tailored to your situation.

In conclusion, starting freelancing with little experience requires a strategic and gradual approach. Building expertise, adjusting rates thoughtfully, focusing on client relationships, and proactively showcasing your skills are key elements. Confidence and a willingness to learn will significantly contribute to your success as a freelancer.

6

Where Do You Find Work?

Best Places To Find Freelance Work: Navigating the Landscape

Finding freelance work is a crucial component of establishing and sustaining a successful freelancing business. In today's digital age, numerous platforms cater to freelancers and clients across a wide array of industries. The key is to choose platforms that not only align with your specific services but also provide access to a pool of potential clients. Let's delve into a more in-depth exploration of popular freelancing platforms and considerations for optimizing your freelance profile.

Consider Your Profile: Elevating Professionalism

Before delving into the intricacies of freelancing platforms, it's paramount to emphasize the significance of a well-crafted profile. Your profile serves as the virtual representation of your professional identity, encompassing details such as your name, skills, qualifications, and a portfolio showcasing your best work. An incomplete or haphazardly assembled profile not only looks unprofessional but can also deter potential clients. Crafting a compelling and comprehensive profile is the first step towards making a positive and lasting impression.

Upwork: Centralized Hub for Opportunities

Upwork stands out as a centralized hub where clients post job listings, detailing project specifics and their freelancer requirements. Freelancers, in turn, submit bids and proposals, presenting themselves as the ideal candidates for the job. The platform streamlines the process of finding work, offering both ease of use and accessibility. However, it's essential to be mindful of the platform's fee structure, as it typically takes a percentage of the payment to cover website fees. Additionally, freelancers often face challenges related to price competition, fostering a "race to the bottom" mentality. Despite these considerations, Upwork remains a widely utilized platform, offering a structured environment for collaboration between clients and freelancers.

Freelancer: Versatility in Job Listings and Communication

Similar to Upwork, Freelancer provides a diverse range of job listings spanning various industries. Clients can review freelancer portfolios before deciding on a collaboration. A notable feature of this platform is its built-in chat system, facilitating seamless communication between clients and freelancers. The platform's versatility and user-friendly interface make it a popular choice among freelancers seeking a broad spectrum of opportunities. As with any freelancing platform, freelancers should be cognizant of potential challenges, including pricing competition and the need to stand out in a crowded marketplace.

Fiverr: Unique Dynamics and Control Over Pricing

Fiverr introduces a unique dynamic to freelancing platforms, particularly in its approach to job postings. Freelancers have the opportunity to showcase their services, allowing clients to browse and select based on the offerings presented. This reverse dynamic empowers freelancers with more control over pricing, and clients can readily discern what fits their budget when browsing project offerings. While competition persists, freelancers on Fiverr have a greater degree of control over the rates they charge for their services.

Guru: Targeting High-Quality Freelancers and Clients

Guru positions itself as a "higher end" freelance work site, specifically targeting expert freelancers and clients seeking top-tier quality. The platform prides itself on creating a more "legitimate" environment, attracting freelancers with a proven track record of excellence. Guru differentiates itself by offering a range of payment options, including traditional fixed-price structures, hourly rates utilizing their time tracking software, and recurring payments for long-term projects. This multi-faceted approach caters to a diverse set of freelancers and clients looking for high-quality collaborations.

Toptal: Vetting for Excellence

Toptal, derived from "top talent," sets itself apart through a rigorous vetting process designed to ensure excellence. Before gaining access to the platform, freelancers undergo experience verification and interviews to verify their expertise. Being part of Toptal not only positions freelancers as top-tier professionals but also attracts high-paying clients seeking top-notch talent. While the exclusivity may limit the number of freelancers on the platform, it creates a curated environment that emphasizes quality over quantity.

iFreelance: Membership-Driven Model and Fee Structure

iFreelance introduces a membership-driven model, offering an alternative to the traditional fee structure prevalent on other platforms. Instead of freelancers relinquishing a portion of each project's earnings as platform fees, iFreelance operates on a monthly membership fee. This model can be advantageous for prolific freelancers who anticipate a high volume of listings. However, the effectiveness of this model depends on the platform's popularity and whether the subscription cost justifies the potential benefits for freelancers.

LinkedIn: Beyond Networking to Professional Opportunities

While primarily known as a professional networking platform, LinkedIn holds untapped potential for freelancers. Beyond updating profiles with new job positions, LinkedIn serves as a powerful tool for building a network of freelancers and potential clients within your industry. Filling out your profile comprehensively, showcasing your work, and providing regular updates on your projects and business activities can significantly enhance your visibility. While setting up a robust LinkedIn profile requires an initial time investment, the potential benefits, including attracting numerous clients and adding value to your freelance business, make it a worthwhile endeavor.

Pitching: Proactive Outreach and Crafting Irresistible Offers

In addition to leveraging freelancing platforms, adopting a proactive pitching strategy can open doors to unique opportunities. Pitching involves reaching out to individuals or organizations with personalized emails, ensuring that you contact the right person and tailor your offer to be irresistible. Personalization and meticulous research into the company's needs are crucial elements of effective pitching. In a landscape inundated with promotional emails, a standout pitch that highlights your unique value proposition is essential. Crafting compelling pitches requires creativity, persistence, and a keen understanding of what sets you apart from the competition.

In conclusion, the freelancing landscape offers diverse platforms catering to different preferences and expertise levels. Selecting the right platforms, optimizing your profile with meticulous detail, and incorporating proactive outreach strategies can significantly enhance your chances of finding lucrative freelance opportunities. Striking a balance between accessibility and quality is key to ensuring sustainable growth in your freelancing business. Remember, each platform has its unique dynamics and challenges, so tailor your approach to align with your business goals and aspirations.

7

How to Advertise Yourself? What's a Portfolio?

How To Advertise Yourself: Crafting an Irresistible Portfolio

A compelling portfolio is the linchpin of a successful freelancing career, serving as a visual testament to your skills, experience, and the value you bring to clients. In the digital age, a portfolio can take the form of a website showcasing your body of work, education, and expertise. Let's delve deeper into the essential elements of building an impactful portfolio and how it contributes to effective self-advertisement.

Defining a Portfolio: Your Freelancer's Showcase

In contemporary freelancing, a portfolio transcends the traditional resume, evolving into a dynamic representation of your capabilities. It encapsulates not only your skills and education but also provides a tangible display of your past projects and achievements. Think of it as a comprehensive snapshot of what you bring to the table, a living document that evolves with each new project and accomplishment.

Building a Portfolio: Transforming Limited Experience into Assets

Clients seek freelancers with a proven track record, and your portfolio plays a pivotal role in establishing credibility. While extensive experience is valuable, showcasing examples of your work can offset any perceived lack of experience. The challenge arises for freelancers with limited experience, and the solution lies in actively seeking opportunities to build a diverse portfolio.

Working for free or at a lower fee is one common strategy for building a portfolio. While this approach may not be suitable for everyone, it can be a stepping stone to accumulating valuable work samples. However, it's crucial to strike a balance, ensuring that your efforts contribute to your long-term goals without compromising the value of your work.

Passion projects also play a significant role. Undertaking projects aligned with your interests allows your passion to shine through in your portfolio, capturing the attention of potential clients who resonate with your enthusiasm. Whether it's a pro bono project for a cause you believe in or a personal project that showcases your unique style, these endeavors contribute to the richness of your portfolio.

Portfolio Content: Showcasing Quality Over Quantity

A well-curated portfolio emphasizes select, high-quality projects that illustrate the depth and scale of your services. Rather than overwhelming clients with an abundance of completed projects, focus on those that best represent your capabilities. Including excerpts of projects can offer a glimpse into your skills without demanding extensive attention.

Consider the narrative your portfolio tells. Each project should not only showcase technical skills but also convey your problem-solving approach, creativity, and adaptability. Craft compelling project descriptions that highlight your role, challenges overcome, and the impact of your contribution. The goal is to provide potential clients with a holistic understanding of your capabilities and how they align with their needs.

Profiles on Websites: Optimizing Information for Client Appeal

When creating profiles on freelancing platforms, comprehensive information is key. Fill out every relevant box or form showcasing your skills, experiences, and examples of your work. Clients often scrutinize these details, making a robust profile instrumental in standing out from the competition.

Highlighting client testimonials on your profiles adds a layer of social proof, reinforcing your reliability and competence. Encourage satisfied clients to leave feedback, creating a positive feedback loop that enhances your online reputation.

Your Website: Beyond Examples of Work

In addition to showcasing your work, your personal website should feature essential information such as contact details. Including relevant experience from your past can bolster your credibility, demonstrating that you bring a wealth of expertise to your freelance endeavors. Some freelancers choose to display rates and packages on their websites, offering transparency to potential clients.

Consider incorporating a blog section on your website. Sharing insights, industry trends, and project case studies not only positions you as an authority in your field but also provides valuable content for potential clients. Regularly updating your blog keeps your website dynamic and signals to clients that you are actively engaged in your industry.

Key sections to incorporate on your website include "About," "Services," "Portfolio," "Testimonials," and "Contact." These sections collectively create a comprehensive overview of your skills, experience, and the services you offer.

Social Media Presence: Amplifying Your Reach

Engaging with social media platforms is a potent strategy for expanding your online presence.

Depending on your service, platforms like Instagram can serve as visual showcases for your work. Starting a blog to share industry insights and experiences is both a portfolio-building and marketing method. Cross-sharing content on platforms like Twitter and Facebook enhances visibility. Tailor your approach based on your business and target audience, ensuring you're present on platforms frequented by potential clients.

In essence, your goal is to be easily found online. Crafting a portfolio that is not only visually appealing but also strategically aligned with your business goals is key to effective self-advertisement in the competitive world of freelancing. As you navigate the intricacies of portfolio development, remember that each piece you showcase is an opportunity to leave a lasting impression on clients and elevate your freelancing career.

8

Where is my Value?

The Importance of Valuing Your Work And Your Time in Freelancing

Determining the right pricing strategy is a common challenge for freelancers. Balancing the need to value your time appropriately with the desire to remain competitive can be intricate. It's crucial to navigate this terrain wisely, recognizing the worth of your skills and time while ensuring your pricing aligns with client expectations.

Navigating Client Expectations: The Rocket and the Moon Analogy

Analogies often simplify complex concepts, and the "rocket to the moon" metaphor vividly captures the dilemma freelancers face. Some clients may demand extensive efforts but offer compensation that doesn't match the scale of the task. The analogy underscores the importance of safeguarding your interests and not succumbing to situations where clients undervalue your expertise.

In a competitive freelancing landscape, there will always be someone willing to work for less. However, setting a fair and comfortable price is essential. Freelancers have living expenses and deserve compensation for their labor. Striking a balance that reflects your expertise and meets your financial needs is pivotal.

Choosing a Niche: The Power of Specialization

Freelancers often grapple with the decision of whether to position themselves as generalists or specialists. Contrary to the belief that being less specific attracts more work, having a niche can confer several advantages. A specialized focus, such as being a finance content writer versus a general content writer, enhances professionalism and instills confidence in potential clients. Over time, establishing a niche allows freelancers to charge premium prices for specialized services.

While it's not mandatory to define your niche immediately, it becomes a strategic move as your freelancing business grows. A well-defined niche not only attracts clients seeking specific expertise but also positions you as an authority in your field.

Time Management: A Cornerstone of Successful Freelancing

Effective time management is not only crucial for productivity but also plays a role in determining pricing. Freelancers need to avoid procrastination and ensure that their working hours are dedicated to productive tasks. While flexibility is a perk of freelancing, it's essential to set clear boundaries to prevent taking undue advantage.

Whether opting for an hourly rate or a project fee, aligning your pricing with your ideal working hours is a personal decision. Motivation and discipline are integral components of successful time management. Implementing organizational techniques, setting deadlines, and providing project updates contribute to staying on task.

Understanding your peak productivity times and structuring your day accordingly enhances efficiency. Tailoring your schedule to capitalize on high-energy periods and incorporating breaks during lulls fosters a balanced and sustainable approach to freelancing.

Value Your Time: The Intersection of Expertise and Compensation

The adage "time is money" encapsulates the principle of valuing your work appropriately. Conducting research on competitors' pricing and industry standards provides a foundation for setting rates. If a project requires additional time or extends beyond the agreed scope, negotiating payment increases is a reasonable step.

Freelancers should resist undervaluing their services, recognizing their expertise and experience as valuable assets. Researching comparable rates and considering long-term financial goals are essential aspects of determining fair compensation. When faced with requests to work for less or for free, freelancers should exercise discernment, understanding their worth and the importance of fair remuneration.

In essence, freelancers are not just service providers but experts in their fields, deserving of equitable compensation for their skills, time, and commitment. Upholding the value of their work ensures not only short-term financial well-being but also contributes to the sustainability and growth of their freelancing careers.

9

How Do I Scale Business?

Transitioning to Full-Time Freelancing: A Leap of Faith

Embarking on a full-time freelance lifestyle is a significant decision that requires careful consideration. The initial stages of freelancing can be unpredictable, with varying workloads and income. Before taking the leap into full-time freelancing, it's advisable to establish a level of security. This involves building a reliable client base, ensuring a steady flow of work, and achieving a comfortable income level. This transitional period allows freelancers to test the waters, gaining insights into the

challenges and opportunities of working independently.

Once you feel confident in your ability to secure clients and maintain a consistent income, the
transition to full-time freelancing becomes a more
viable and less risky endeavor. This leap of faith is
about dedicating yourself entirely to your freelance
career, seizing the opportunity to fully immerse
yourself in the freelancing world.

Building a Freelance Team: Collaboration and Expansion

Contrary to the misconception that freelancers
must work in isolation, there's an option to build
a team. Hiring others can enhance your business
capabilities, enabling you to offer a broader range
of services or delegate tasks to a team with comple-
mentary skills. This expansion could involve growing your business offerings or having a team of
individuals performing similar roles.

Collaboration within a team fosters creativity,

efficiency, and the ability to take on larger projects. It also allows freelancers to focus on their core strengths while leveraging the expertise of team members in other areas. As a result, the freelance business becomes a collective effort, potentially leading to increased productivity and a more robust service offering.

Subcontracting: Outsourcing for Business Efficiency

If managing a team isn't your preference or doesn't align with your business model, subcontracting specific tasks or services is an alternative strategy. Outsourcing elements like business administration, marketing, or accounting to virtual assistants or specialists can streamline your operations.

Subcontracting allows freelancers to maintain a lean operation while accessing expertise in specific areas. This approach is particularly beneficial for freelancers who prefer a hands-on approach to their core services while delegating supplementary tasks to external professionals.

Niche Specialization: Tailoring Your Services for Success

Narrowing your freelance services down to a niche can significantly benefit your business. Clients often prefer specialists, such as a finance writer, over generalists. Specialization not only makes you more appealing to your target audience but also positions you to charge premium prices for your expertise.

Choosing a niche involves identifying your unique strengths and aligning them with market demands. It allows freelancers to become authorities in their chosen field, establishing credibility and trust among clients seeking specialized services. This strategic focus contributes to the overall success and sustainability of a freelance business.

Building a Brand: Establishing Reputability and Authority

As your freelancing career progresses, creating a cohesive brand becomes a valuable asset. While not essential for all freelancers, a well-defined brand enhances your reputation and authority in the marketplace. Building a brand involves crafting a consistent and professional image that resonates with your target audience.

Elements of brand-building include a compelling visual identity, a clear mission statement, and a unique value proposition. Effective branding communicates your personality, values, and the quality of your services. Clients often prefer working with individuals who project authenticity and professionalism, making brand development an essential aspect of long-term success in freelancing.

Diversifying Services: Expanding Your Business Horizons

To keep your business dynamic and responsive to client demands, consider adding new services.

This could involve introducing new elements to your existing packages or exploring different facets of your industry. Adapting to evolving client needs ensures that your business remains relevant and competitive in the ever-changing freelancing landscape.

Diversification allows freelancers to explore additional revenue streams and cater to a broader clientele. It requires a strategic approach, including market research, skill development, and a keen understanding of emerging trends in the industry. By expanding services thoughtfully, freelancers position themselves to capture a more extensive market share and foster long-term business growth.

Price Adjustments: Recognizing Your Worth and Experience

As you accumulate more experience and skills, it's crucial to reassess and adjust your pricing accordingly. Recognize the value of your hard work and expertise by increasing your prices. This step not only reflects your growing proficiency but also contributes to your financial well-being.

Determining appropriate pricing involves considering factors such as market rates, your level of expertise, and the unique value you bring to clients. Conducting market research and staying informed about industry standards helps freelancers make informed decisions about their pricing strategy. Clients who appreciate the quality of your work are often willing to pay higher rates for your services, contributing to the overall sustainability and success of your freelance business.

In essence, the freelancing journey is a dynamic and evolving process. Whether you choose to build a team, subcontract tasks, specialize in a niche, build a brand, diversify services, or adjust prices, the key is to adapt and grow in response to your experiences and the changing landscape of freelancing. Each strategic move contributes to the resilience and longevity of a freelance career.

10

A Couple Final Words

Navigating the Freelance Journey

Starting a freelance business is a journey filled with challenges, opportunities, and the freedom to shape your professional life. As you embark on this path, consider the following key takeaways:

1. Prioritize Your Portfolio:

Your portfolio is your strongest advertising tool. Craft an outstanding portfolio that showcases your skills, experience, and the quality of your work. It serves as a visual representation of your capabilities to potential clients.

2. Define Your Service and Audience:

Clearly define your freelance service and target audience. Ensure that your services align with the needs of your audience, making your business relevant and attractive to potential clients.

3. Build Skills and Credibility:

Take on projects, even if they are not ideal, to build your skills, gain valuable experience, and establish credibility in your field. The early stages of freelancing are about honing your craft and proving your capabilities.

4. Business Operations:

Focus on the business side of your freelance venture. Ensure that your operations are legal and compliant. Attend to administrative tasks, financial management, and legal considerations to operate as a professional and legitimate business entity.

5. Identify Client Hotspots:

When transitioning to full-time freelancing, identify the best places to find clients. Frequent these platforms, advertise effectively, and develop strategies to connect with your target audience. Establish a strong online presence to enhance visibility.

6. Time Management and Productivity:

Maximize the flexibility of freelancing by mastering time management and productivity. Develop routines, set clear working hours, and leverage your flexibility to work in a way that suits your preferences while maintaining peak productivity.

7. Scale Your Business:

As your freelance business gains traction, consider scaling it up. You have the autonomy to decide how and when your business operates. Explore opportunities to expand your service offerings, collaborate with a team, or subcontract tasks to enhance efficiency.

8. Enjoy the Freelance Journey:

Despite the challenges, relish the unique benefits of freelance work. It offers unparalleled flexibility and the opportunity to live life on your terms. Embrace the freedom that comes with being your own boss, and find joy in the liberating and rewarding aspects of freelancing.

9. Ensure Longevity with Planning:

Keep a close eye on industry trends, continuously update your skills, and monitor your progress. Plan your freelance business strategically, adapting your approach as your business evolves. Longevity in freelancing comes from careful planning, staying informed, and being adaptable to change.

In conclusion, while freelance work is demanding, the potential rewards make it a fulfilling and liberating career choice. By putting in the effort, planning diligently, and staying attuned to industry dynamics, your freelance business can thrive, providing you with the opportunity to live your dream life. Freelancing is a journey that requires dedication, but the freedom it offers is truly unparalleled.

Video Courses:

Podcasting 101: https://www.youtube.com/playlist?list=PLkDvo91I6DB-CaP_m0VoXtsI2YtWIQ8XjA

Membership Masterclass: https://www.youtube.com/playlist?list=PLkDvo91I6DBA-JtQzU5OW8l3Zk42PlUMv1

Books

Maximize Your Podcast for Low Cost: https://amzn.to/3v1VSHT

Bald and Bonkers Network LLC offers memberships through it's company YouTube channel and Patreon Page that offer books and exclusive courses to members. Members could also get exclusive updates to new projects and more! All funds are used to advance company operations and offer new opportunities for creators of all types.